A Leap of Faith

Inala Bruce-Rose

Presentation by *BookLeaf Publishing*

Web: www.bookleafpub.com

E-mail: info@bookleafpub.com

ISBN: 9789358738469

First edition 2023

*To my family, friends, and others in my life
who have supported me and believed in me,
thank you.*

ACKNOWLEDGEMENT

I'd like to acknowledge the people in my life dear to my heart who I've lost. May they rest in peace, and thank you for every step and every moment you were a part of.

Table of Contents

Stranger

You're unfamiliar to me
The way you encase me with your beauty truly
Restoring my poor eyesight so that I can see
I'm blinded sometimes, always, usually?

You crept into my heart, soul, and mind,
Like an assassin you caught me from behind
Who told you to invade my thoughts and stay
Knowing you're there scares me, I run away?

The dark forest around me never knew you
And yet I'm under your spell sealed with a kiss
You came right in like a gust of wind blew
My dark forest starting to die? Gosh what bliss

You have no business being in my forest but I
can't let you go

You see, you're no longer a stranger so...
You invaded like a wildfire and those are hard to diffuse
I guess in the end you left me no choice but to choose

You....Stranger

Breathe

Inhale, 1, 2, 3, exhale…4, 5, 6…
One deep breath…one trouble gone
Inhale deep thoughts.. Exhale anxiety
Two deep breaths… two troubles gone
Inhale…wait who am I kidding?
How many times has someone told you, just
breathe?
Breathe…from the word breath
Breathe a breath of fresh air,
Breathe in good vibes, breathe out intrusive
thoughts
Breathe?
Am I breathing for me or for you?
INHALE DEEP, like a newborn babe
EXHALE like the wind on a violent day
How can you breathe when your mind is
cluttered
Like entangled vines
How can you breathe when there's a violent fire
inside?
How can you breathe when there's nowhere to
hide?
In and out, in and out, in and out, in….and…
out….

It's hard to breathe when your mind goes at
lightning speed
It's hard to breathe when your body shivers like
it jumped into the sea
It's hard to breathe when your palms are sweaty
and feel like 100 degrees
It's HARD!
What's harder than finding your center, your
ground, your sanity, your..self?
Breathe with nature's ocean waves
Breathe and feel the sun's beautiful rays
Breathe under the stars and moonlight
Breathe….take that breath
Breathe in 1, 2, 3…hold it…gather those
thoughts
Breathe out 4, 5, 6….pause…take that moment
Be present, just… breathe….

Lost

My mind is like a Bermuda Triangle
Sometimes something goes in but it never comes
out
It's easy to step in and get lost
There are multiple electrical fences and locked
doors, and to top it all off it's after you pass the
brick wall
It's hard to get out of my lost thoughts where the
fog exists so thick you can hardly see through it

Sometimes I get in a daze and daydream so
much I forget where reality is

Sometimes when you're lost it's hard to find
your way back, like an escaped pet far from
home
It feels like a hidden treasure that you will never
find
Sometimes you have to get lost in order to be
found again
So to my younger self, we were once lost, but I
promise every step of the way I am finding us
again
We are no longer just lost

I Didn't Know...

I didn't know that saying no to your space being
invaded was not an issue
I didn't know that sticking up for yourself and
having boundaries would cause tears and tissues
I didn't know that your own body can feel
foreign to you
I didn't know that just one touch can lead to
more than two
I didn't know that wasn't the definition of love
I didn't know that I'd feel dirty and keep looking
for answers above
I didn't know that giving in and being silent
would cause so much harm
I didn't know a touch could feel so wrong on my
arm
I didn't know how to speak up and ask for
advice
I didn't know that my heart could turn cold like
ice
I didn't know how to realize what had been done
I didn't know what I didn't know but that
doesn't mean they've won
I didn't know I'd feel whole again and free
I didn't know that advocating for yourself could
feel so good and feel like me

Next time that you don't know don't be quiet
speak up and be firm
Because despite all the things I didn't know, I
know I've learned

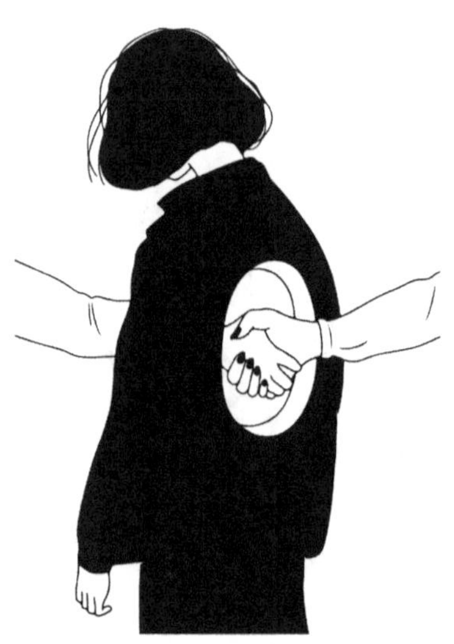

I Am Not My Hair

I am not my hair
The way I represent my culture with thick
beautiful curls should not affect my appearance
of being professional
I am not my hair
The way that I decide to wear twists one day or
braids the other should not allow you to criticize
my intelligence
I am not my hair
My hair length should not be used to question
my beauty because my beautiful is within not
just out
I am not my hair
The way my luscious fro is let wild and free
does not mean I don't care because it seems
"Undone, or unfavorable"
I am not my hair
If a wig is laid on top of my braids whose
business are you minding for I am merely
protecting what's underneath
I am not my hair
The color of my hair is none of your concern
because that does not determine my skill set or
maturity
I am not my hair

Telling me to straighten my hair just to look
professional does not mean my natural look
should be discouraged
I AM NOT …MY HAIR
Please don't judge me for how I choose to wear
my hair because my hair does not define who I
am it is a part of me
And that part of me is deep-rooted within my
soul

I Wish I'd Known

You sat across from me, but I gave it no mind
During that time my thoughts raced, in a bind
Eventually your smile graced my presence and
embraced me, devoured me whole
Your hello that followed allowed me to glimpse
your soul
I wish I'd known…

Days, weeks, months went by and your heart
warmed mine
As time flew by your pain and cries grew larger
and you responded to how are you doing with
I'm doing fine
When in reality that was a tact to keep your fear
and sorrow from taking over

I wish I'd known….
I saw through your mask of deception, we
discussed and I was there but still that smile
gave me hope
The way you explained your struggles and
challenges felt like you were tied to a tree by a
rope

Yet, it still wasn't enough, you would tug and
pull and tug and pull and tug and pull, but to no
avail
Sometimes you'd describe it as if it was your
personal hell
I WISH I'D KNOWN!

As seasons shifted, so did our bond
It expanded and grew from a puddle to a pond
From a pond to a river and a river to a lake
From a lake to a broken heart that aches
I.. Wish.. I'd known

From first day of school to Halloween
To snow falls and Xmas movie scenes
To Merry Christmas everyone and Happy
holidays
To I'm in pain in so many ways
To I'm okay now guys it was just a scare
To goodbye guys as I'm no longer there
To instant shock and denial, and a room full of
blank stares
To tears that continue to fall down like Niagara
on faces bare
To racing minds and last words
To hugs and sorry for your losses and paintings
of birds
To one final thought left pondering

So many people around but I tune them out and
I'm left wondering

What would've happened and what more would
I have done
If only just if only I had a small glimpse
Instead of sitting here saying to myself
i wish.. i'd known….

Alone

Alone
Alone is being surrounded by a group of people
but still feeling like you're the only one there
Alone is sitting in silence deep in thought
Alone is talking to people all day, but yet still
feeling empty inside
Alone is misunderstandings of who you are and
how you feel
Alone is not a place, but a feeling inside your
heart that gets harder and harder to fill
Alone is what you define as alone and no one
else
It's ok to feel alone…

Dear Self?

Dear self?
Dear self, or me, or you no that's not right…
Dear Inala, dear… wow this is hard…again I'll
get it this time
Dear little Nala, all I can say is we are making
our dreams come true one step at a time
Wait! Oh shoot this was supposed to be to future
adult Nala
Let's go again… (clears throat)
But wait, don't I have to cater to all parts of me?
Past, present, future?
Future is nothing without present and present is
nothing without past right?
Hmmm..
Dear future Nala..

I am writing to you to simply say, our past scars
are being sutured shut, our present heart beats
with love and hope, and we took this chance so
that the future you will never be afraid to take a
leap of faith again…

Love, past, present and in the future, yourself

Naked

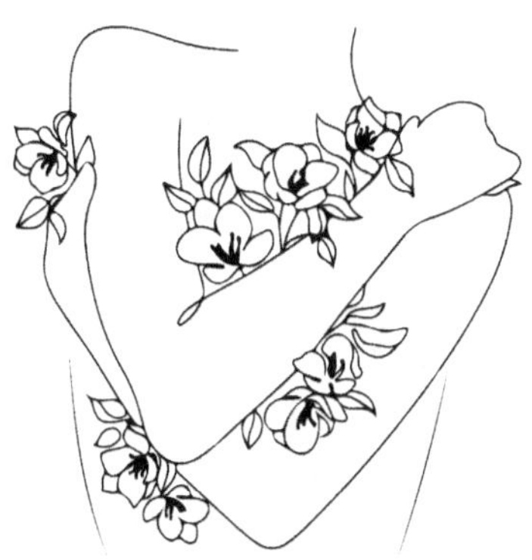

When you're born into this world do you have
clothes or are you naked?
Are you free until someone tells you you're not?
Are you born thinking about who likes you?
Who's talking about you in a negative light and
who doesn't like you?
Are you born with a personality that just wants
to be?
Does your identity feel lost or misplaced?
When you think about these questions I hope the
answer to them are clear to you.
Naked, what comes to mind when you hear the
word naked?

Is it a nude human being?
Is it you being bare to share your soul with
another?

Is it an unfinished piece that has yet to tell its
story?
Naked
I think of a vulnerable human being
A person that wants to strip themselves bare of
labels and ridicule
Judgment and spite
Anger and madness
Sadness and strife

A person that wants nothing more than to strip
their identities, and many hats, just to wear one
The one that includes the ability to be
themselves
And not have to hide and cloak themselves with
the melting pot of society
A person that stands out like the black sheep in
the herd
Naked
When you feel comfortable in your own skin
like a banana in its peel
Or when you shed the negativity like reptiles to
become born and new again
Naked

Just be you in all your glory
Don't wear clothes that don't fit
Everything is not made or meant for everyone so
it's ok to find what fits

You should feel free, one with your skin
Not like a foreign entity coming for a visit
Love yourself inside and out and feel that
comfort
Learn to love.. being.. naked

Feelings Are Like Hallways with Infinite Doors...

Feelings are like hallways with infinite doors
You take a step on the dark, white, or clear
floors
Walk down that hallway turn left or right
But beware of what could be in your sight
You could touch a knob and be frozen to the
touch
Or open a door and get swooped into its clutch
You can burn up in the flames and heat up
piping hot
Or you could give into temptation and all
morality turns to rot
You could bounce from door to door confused
on where to go
You could step inside an Icy storm with inches
of snow
You could easily stay in the hallway feeling all
alone
Or simply get lost in a completely other zone
Round and round and round all day
When you awake it's a random array
You never know what you'll get; the possibilities
are endless

Just watch out because some hallways have
doors whose effects are tremendous

Nature's Emotions

It's late at night
The crickets are out, the birds sound asleep
The wind is alive, swooshing past cars, homes,
buildings, windows
All was quiet until…
BOOM, CRACK, (knock, knock)
Clouds make their entrance
They start to weep

Pitter patter, the tears hit the window slow
Then aggressively creating endless puddles and
reflections of pain
First came the scream, it screeched so loud!
Then came the tears and gasps for air
A warm hug wraps her in its arms til the
weeping and screaming stops

Creaaakkkk (the door opens) the clouds leave
Knock, knock.. another guest?
Who is it?
The knocking stops
BANG BANG BANG!
Banging but who?
Check the thermostat, all the tears are now dry
Sizzling hot to the touch, the boiling point has
been reached and finally chose to erupt
Who is it? I am blinded before an answer comes,
so hot and so bright
But wait, is that another guest in the distance?
This guest is ice cold, so cold that it traps the
guest from before with clouds and the wind
roars, picking up anything in its way
Shivers go down my spine, and creatures start to
hide
Because this guest is like Medusa
If you get too close you'll be frozen
The doors are rock hard solid and frozen shut
CRUNCH, the sound of my feet when I open the
door
This was the last guest, Ice cold
You can feel the silence
The guest stays awhile until it's time to go and
then the cycle repeats itself again
Nature's emotions

Letting Go

Letting go is hard to do
When something aches your heart so bad that
you feel like your breath is being sucked out of
your body and your heart pounds back and forth
like a drum in a drum line
You feel lost, resentful, hurt, angry, envious, the
list goes on
Letting go is the mature thing to do, but what no
one tells you is that you sometimes have to let
go for you and not them
When you let something go or someone, it's so
hard but in the end you'll understand why
Time does heal but healing takes time
And healing hurts before it gets better like a
deep wound or injury to your body
Some nights you're gasping for air, like
someone punched you in the chest with all their
might
and others your smile is big from ear to ear to
mask the pain
Letting go is necessary in life, but that doesn't
mean it hurts less
And sometimes you have to let go to get
yourself together because if you're not whole
how can you pour into someone else's cup?

Letting go isn't a negative thing but allowing
there to be room for improvement or a content
feeling in life
Letting go may be hard to do, but in life what
isn't?

The Heart

Close your eyes
Breathe in deep and slowly exhale
Keep your eyes closed
Focus on your ears
Do you hear that?
Try focusing on the sound of your heartbeat
Now take your hand
Place it on your heart
Can you hear it now and feel it?
When you feel alone, lost, anxious whatever it
may be
Take the time to feel and listen to your heart
It has something to say always…

The Good Girl

You must remain perfect
Pause the word perfect
Meaning everything must remain in place
Hair, nails, body, face, attitude, hormones,
attention, clothes, focus, need I go on?
Ok check got it
What are you crying for?
Oh this… what should I say oh..my..god..
Ummm ooh I know, let's say nothing I'll be ok
Great answer bravo
You sure?
Yea I'm sure
Pretend you're a princess
Smile and wave
Stand up straight

That outfit is too loose, this one is too tight
Showing skin is unacceptable
You must remain intelligent
No grades below a b as a c is an f and a b is
room for improvement
You have to try harder
Do not argue
Your opinion can be stated, however watch who
you're talking to
Remain poise and elegant
No tackling, no video games, no shouting, shhhh
you're too loud
Don't dress for attention if you don't want it
Don't talk with your mouth full
Don't eat too much you'll gain weight
Oh how can I forget, you should be presentable
every second of the day
Honestly, who am I kidding these standards in
place for society change so often
You're too fat, you're too skinny
You're too dark, you're too light
You're too wild, you're too quiet
You're not sexy enough, you're too sexy
You're too tall, you're too short
DOES IT EVER END??!!
Being the ideal "good girl" is hard
So, I say screw these standards and just be you,
the girl you were meant to be
Perfectly imperfect is my motto

Shoes

Have you ever heard of the phrase
Take a walk in their shoes?
Well it's true, you never know what someone
else is going through until you walk the same
steps they do and wear their shoes
That angry boss that always snaps at you
Your severely depressed coworker
The person that always smiles and you don't
know why
The tears that fall from someone's face
Or the pure silence that's filled with hatred for
another
Shoes are all different sizes, styles, colors,
materials, but not one shoe is the same

Next time you want to judge someone for being
overweight, too skinny, their scars, their teeth,
their feelings
Just take a second to try to walk in their shoes or
think about them, because one day your shoes or
someone you care about could feel the same

Time

What is the definition of time?
Those Infinite Minutes do not Exist
Because see time waits for no one
Time does not wait when you are running late
for work
Time does not wait when you have homework to
do but life smacked you hard and knocked you
on your face
Time does not wait for us to be kind to our loved
ones before they depart from Earth
Time does not wait for your heart to break
For you to lose everything and gain more
Time is not fair and nor is it equivalent all over
the world

Time can go slow or fast but that depends on
you
Tick tock tick tock, time alerts you how to start
your day and plan it
Tick tock tick tock.. time for self-care, some
rest, a break, to leave.. time keeps going with or
without you
So just be kind and cherish your time

Layers

Humans are like onions with many layers
And even when one is lost there's always
another
There are various parts to a human soul
Each layer reveals more and more about
someone
On the outside is the barrier that protects what's
within
But you'll never know what's within just by
looking at the outside
Ever heard of don't judge a book by its cover?
Don't judge a person by the skin that they are in
The soul is the core piece of a human and
without it lies an empty shell of a person
Tacos are empty without the layers of toppings
that go on them
A home cannot be built just with tools alone,
you have to have the materials necessary to help
build
Without layers of the world the core would burn
us all alive
Without layers in the sky we would be subject to
an unfathomable demise
Point is, layers hold an essential part to our lives
and every layer was not meant to be like another

So before you judge someone
Try to think of their layers
You never know what you might find

Reflection

A mirror can only show you what's in front of it
It doesn't alter what it sees, but those who look
within distort the image they see
A mirror Can reflect what's inside and out
Your face can swell as tears escape your eyes
Or it can crease together from laughter and a
smile
Reflections can't lie
They tell you the truth regardless of if you ask
for it or not
Am I taking good enough care of myself?
Do I look like hell?
Am I enough?
Sitting in front of a mirror can do a lot from
giving us a pep talk

Practice having difficult conversations
Self-reflection
Making difficult decisions
Practice for that performance or speech you're
nervous about
So
What does your reflection do for you?
What do you see when you look deep within and
stare at your reflection?

Life is Like a Game of Chess

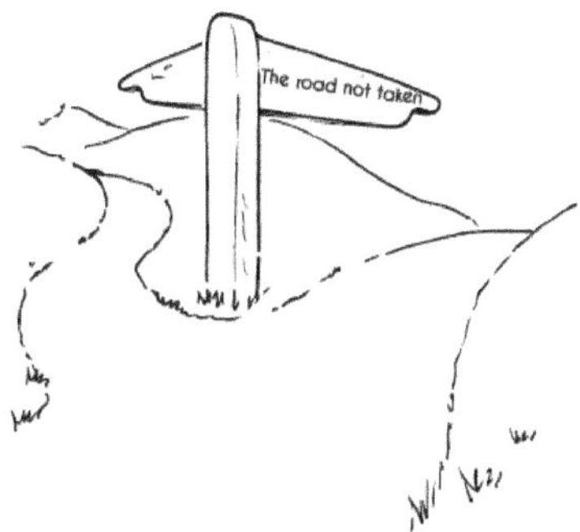

Life is like a game of chess
If you're not careful about which choice you
make, it can cause a domino effect of events
Life is like a game of chess
You have multiple options laid out in front of
you but eventually it becomes one path for you
to take, that you possibly can't miss
Life is like a game of chess
There is a strategy and some choices take deeper
thought than others
However your end goal ends up being the same
Life is like a game of chess
Sometimes there are sacrifices to be made for
the greatest outcome to reveal itself
Life is like a game of chess

It was never meant to be easy, but you learn until
you're able to make better choices even when
you make mistakes
Life is like a game of chess because if you're not
careful you may lose it all and it's not worth
losing yourself